42-0

The Story of Four Extraordinary Seasons

John Fairless

Copyright © 2016 John Fairless

All rights reserved.

ISBN: **069281664X**
ISBN-13: **978-0692816646**

Dedication

To the victorious Panthers and Chargers, heroes of my youth.
To a small town that was a great place to grow up.
To the parents, teachers, and leaders that made it so.
"Magnitudo insit singulis, si tamen audet somniare."

CONTENTS

CONTENTS

The Snap, the Hold, the Kick 3

Chapter One: The Beginning 7

Chapter Two: Transition 19

Chapter Three: The Streak Begins 25

Chapter Four: Cogs in the Machine 31

Chapter Five: Growth and Change 37

Chapter 6: Cold's Not the Word for It 47

Chapter 7: The Path for a Champion 55

Chapter 8: Destiny Awaits 63

Chapter 9: The Game 75

Chapter 10: One More – and an Epilogue 87

A Picture Gallery 91

ACKNOWLEDGMENTS

The passion to tell this story goes back to my own days as a young person growing up in Martin, Tennessee. I loved my little town, and have grown to appreciate it all the more as the years have gone by and I have lived in lots of other places.

A Facebook conversation with Julia White Brundige was the spark that ignited the flame, as she told of people who come up to her husband, Johnny (aka, The Toe) and ask about the field goal that won the Humboldt game to this day.

Conversations ensued with a number of distinguished gentlemen and ladies, without whose help this book would not have been possible: Phil Dane, Johnny Shanklin, Linda Neese Culver, Johnny and Julia Brundige, Kenny Winstead, Danny and Susan Walker, Mark Stafford, Barry Buckley, Don Jacobs, Walter Benson, Randy Brundige, Joe Page, Julia Terry, Larry Washburn, Rick Wilson, Brenda Whitlow, Richard Bragg – and if I have forgotten anybody else, please forgive me! I could not have possibly included every great story I heard.

I would especially like to thank Coach Jim Graves and his wife, Glenda, for allowing me to come sit in their home and converse. I owe both of you a great deal.

The work of Dr. Hobart Beale, dedicated football fan and historian, was absolutely invaluable to the foundation of my own book. Without Dr. Beale's exhaustive treatment, *Panthers : Martin High School, 1924-1969 : 45 years of MHS Football*, my research trail would have been much longer. Ditto for the assistance I received from Randy Cavin, Sports Editor, and the staff of the *Weakley County Press* – whose pages I continue to read every chance I get, a habit of many years.

Finally, I have waited more than 40 years to type these words of appreciation for two English teachers who exemplified the excellence we enjoyed as students in our Martin public schools: for Joan Pritchett, because you first told me that I could write a book one day, and for Jenna Wright – because you told me that I would!

The Snap, the Hold, the Kick

Things go wrong in football all the time.

Players line up out of position; linemen block the wrong defender, or miss a block completely. Backs run right instead of left, fumbles are lost, players get hurt; heck, even coaches get confused about what is supposed to happen.

But no other play in football is as likely to have a mix-up as the attempt for a field goal

It's an odd play in which the center – who is bent over, looking back between his legs -- must manage to snap the ball precisely seven yards to a holder who is kneeling, with his hands in the air. The holder must catch the ball and place it, end down, onto a small piece of plastic, approximately 4-inches square, resting on the ground. The laces of the football must be turned so that the foot of the kicker can impact the leather of the ball in the best possible location.

The kicker times his approach to the ball, aiming to strike it with his foot just as the opposing team rushes toward him to block the kick –

if they can. If the ball clears the goal post, the kick is good. The whole play is over in a matter of a few seconds.

In a game filled with runs, passes, touchdowns, and extra points – all plays that are exciting in their own right – it is amazing how many times a game is decided by the attempt of a field goal.

> (Case in point: the NFL record for game-winning field goals is held by Morten Anderson, who did it 35 times. He also <u>missed</u> 134 kicks in his career.)

Even great players fold under the pressure of making a kick when the game is "on the line."

On a Friday night in November of 1970, in a small Tennessee town, there were 10,000 people watching – waiting, wondering – to see if a field-goal try was going to mean a victory dance for one undefeated high school team, and a "walk of shame" for another. Two communities laid their pride on the line; passions were high and tempers were, too.

The Chargers of Martin-Westview High School[*] were proud possessors of a brand-new state record for consecutive victories: 40 games in a row had gone their way over the past four seasons. The Rams of Humboldt High School were also undefeated in the 1970 season, and were the team with the higher ranking and all the expectations for success on this night.

---

[*] In a later chapter, the nature of the two schools – three, actually – that are a part of this name is explained.

Interest was so intense that other high school teams rescheduled their games that week, and bus- and carloads of observers from the surrounding towns packed the stadium to watch these two teams battle it out.

With: 08 seconds on the game clock and the score tied 20-20, the hometown Chargers lined up to attempt the field goal.

If you wanted to script a perfect ending for a movie-type moment, you would have the coach calling time out, gathering his team for a final, stirring speech about "giving your all" and making "just one more great play for the fans," or some such. The team would run on to the field, calmly line up for the play, the ball would be snapped and the kick would sail into the air.

A few agonizing, slow-motion frames later, the outcome would be revealed with dramatic music blaring and bright lights blazing.

Success. Defeat. Distilled in a single play, a crystalline moment of ecstasy and agony.

In real life, things rarely happen like that.

This is the story of how a football team – four of them, actually – came to symbolize hope and a white-knuckled determination to keep things together in a time when the world was coming apart at the seams.

In the closing years of the 1960's, Americans fought over racial integration, protested an unpopular war in Vietnam, and witnessed the assassinations of political and religious leaders. School children practiced bomb drills and citizens wondered if the American way of life "as they knew it" was going to end. The world was coming closer every day, and it felt like a dangerous place to be.

With all of that going on, just how important could a field goal and a football game be?

I invite you to a time that is now suspended in memory, separated from the reality of modern life and our daily grind – yet which remains as touchable and tangible as the things we experienced only yesterday.

Maybe – for some of us – they are more real than that.

Maybe – a kick means more than winning or losing a game.

Chapter One: The Beginning

Perfection is hard to achieve in any sport; not very many football teams ever get to go undefeated for an entire season. For the Martin High School Panthers of 1967, there were several moments where the magic almost didn't happen.

I was a kid in the stands, watching the games with my dad in those days. I remember how awed I was by the blue and white uniforms the "big boys" got to wear. Those guys were like gods, descended from the clouds as mighty warriors. Though they were only in high school, they all looked 7-feet tall and stronger than Superman to me.

The names of the starters are emblazoned in my memories: Mike Beeler, senior quarterback; Richard Bragg, the hard-charging fullback who always seemed able to get "three yards and a cloud of dust" when you needed it.

Bobby Morrison was the speedy tailback, a player that many remembered as "pound for pound the toughest guy on the field." Barry Harper and George Crawford complemented Morrison and Bragg perfectly; the Martin ground attack wore opponents out all season long.

Then, there were the linemen – the guys who played tough, but rarely got the glory. I was drawn to the action there "in the trenches," even then; I thought it was cool that the guys on the line got to hit somebody on every play. Across the front in 1967, the movers and shakers were Danny Nanney, Alan Hazelwood, Jackie Stanfill, and Joe Martin. Larry Harper and Mickey McAdoo covered the ends.

This starting 11 gained crucial support from other substitute players over the course of 11 games. A season is something of a living organism, in and of itself; there are rhythms and pulses, accidents and injuries. Any player will tell you that the team is never the same by the end of the year as they were when they began. That was never truer than with the team that was the 1967 Martin Panthers.

In the Fall of 1966, one year earlier, public schools in Tennessee had been racially integrated for the first time. With heretofore "separate but equal" facilities – often on the opposite sides of town – no one was sure exactly what would happen when whites and blacks showed up to attend the same schools.

Martin, Tennessee is a small town in a rural county in western Tennessee – about 10 miles from the Kentucky border and 25 miles or so from the Mississippi River. It was certainly not a hotbed of racial activity in those days, but that didn't mean the town's residents weren't a little nervous, themselves.

"I remember wondering what would happen when I showed up at the white school," says Julia Terry, who was attending fifth grade in 1966. "I thought maybe I would be spit on, or that I might get hit."

Larry Washburn, an eighth-grader that year, remembers being nervous about attending the new junior high school – which was housed in the former Weakley County Educational Center – the black school. "There was some tension; there were rumors of kids getting shoved around in the bathrooms, stuff like that."

Weeks before the other kids hit the hallways at school, though, the members of the football team reported for preseason, two-a-day workouts. Martin High School had 39 players on the roster for the season; three of them were black.

"I don't ever remember a problem, not even from the first day," says Johnny Shanklin, one of the three. "We were all there to play ball – that's what we wanted to do, and that's what was important. So I guess we just decided to play and let that be that."

Head Coach Jim Graves was known for putting his players through a pretty rough regimen. It didn't matter to him what the color of a player's skin was. As long as a man was willing to run, tackle, practice hard, listen and learn – he had a chance to be a ballplayer, and they had a chance to be a good team.

Coach Graves was tough; everybody knew that. But he was also keenly interested in the development of his players, not only in their athletic ability but in every area of their lives. "I want you men to be the leaders in this school," one player said, remembering one of the coach's speeches to the team. "Go to class, make your grades, treat your teachers and your classmates with respect. And always remember that, if it's worth doing – it's worth doing right **the first time!**"

"I would have run through a wall for that man," Shanklin added.

Graves' 1966 Panther football team had had a good year, winning 7 games while losing 3. The last game of the year was a nail-biter, as they lost by a single point to one of their most-heated rivals, the Dresden Lions.

Now, as the '67 season got underway, that 7-6 score was plastered in the minds of the players who came back; long before the days of press clippings pinned to locker room billboards, that score was all the motivational material they would need in the season that was about to unfold.

The first win in that perfect season came at home against arch-rivals Union City. The Panthers got three touchdowns from Barry Harper, one from Morrison, and one from young Johnny Shanklin (a sign of great things to come.) They easily outdistanced the Golden Tornado, 32-13.

So far, so good. But one game does not a season make.

Things immediately got tougher as Martin crossed the state line to take on Fulton, Kentucky – a team that had dealt them their only significant defeat a season earlier (that one ended with Fulton on top 19-0.) The only score of the night was by Bobby Morrison on a 7-yard touchdown run, with Barry Harper adding the extra point. The Martin defense was the difference, as three different Panthers (Crawford, McAdoo, and Beeler) intercepted passes. The final score was 7-0 and Martin High School had now won two games in a row.

Up next was South Fulton, Tennessee – which just so happened to be the only other team to have beaten Martin the previous season (also 7-6.) Revenge belonged to the Panthers on this night, however, by a score of 28-0, with rushing touchdowns from Morrison, Bragg, and Beeler (who had two.)

Three in a row – but nobody calls that a streak. Especially Coach Graves, who was determined to keep his players focused on one game at a time. The steely-jawed former Navy submariner was absolutely committed to team discipline; it did not matter if a player was one of the stars or a third-string water boy.

An incident with star running back Bobby Morrison illustrates the point.

Jim Graves, in many ways, both defined and defied the stereotype of the tough, hard-nosed football coach in those days. Though he was intense, one of his principles was that there was absolutely no cursing allowed on the team. He set the example, as multiple players remembered, "I never heard a foul word come out his mouth."

Morrison, whose fiery temper matched the intensity with which he played the game, was struggling at practice one afternoon. After a certain disappointing play, he uttered a practically unforgivable curse that invoked damnation in the name of the Deity. Graves' eyes nearly popped out of his head; the veins on his neck stood rigid as he screamed at Morrison, "Get off of my field; get out of here. I don't ever want to see you back!"

Morrison was shocked, as were his teammates. After all, Bobby played both ways (offense and defense) and was a key member of the team. With him out of the lineup, the Panthers' chances of winning were significantly reduced.

As Phil Dane, who was observing practice as an eighth-grader that day remembers it, Morrison ran to the locker room, intending to take off his equipment and change into his street clothes. However, the door was locked and he couldn't get inside. So, while the team continued to work out, Bobby sat down and cried. That's where the team managers found him when they came to open the door at the end of practice.

Morrison began to beg and plead with the coach, apologizing profusely. Graves would not yield. Morrison was off the team. In the days that followed, several the team members urged the coach to have some leniency. After a meeting with Morrison, Coach Graves did indeed let Bobby return to the team, though as his penance, he would have to run "grass drills" after practice each day.

> (The grass drill involves a player running continually and falling to the ground every time the coach blows the whistle; you must immediately get back up and continue running until the next whistle blows. That cycle repeats itself as long as the coach feels you need to keep running. Players despise running grass drills.)

Phil Dane finishes the story: "Bobby ran grass drills for a very long time after that!"

Two more easy victories came against Gleason and Sharon and the season was half-way over; Martin was 5-0.

If anybody was thinking of going undefeated all year long at that point, they were keeping it to themselves, as the next game would pit the Panthers against a team they loved to hate. (I'm sure the feeling was mutual!)

The Falcons of Lake County came to Martin with upset on their minds. Martin scored first on a run by Mike Beeler and an extra point by Johnny Shanklin. But it was the Falcons that dazzled the crowd and stunned the home stadium into silence for the next three quarters. After three straight touchdown drives, Lake County led the game by a score of 20-7. Martin had not been down by this kind of margin all season long.

Fighting for their lives, the Panthers could not make headway against the Lake County defense. In the fourth quarter, with another drive stalling and Martin in danger of watching their undefeated season go up in flames, Coach Jim Graves decided to risk the game on a fourth down with 1 yard to go. The call went to #33, the Panther fullback – Richard Bragg.

As Johnny Shanklin remembers it, "Bragg would rather fight than eat, and he wasn't about to let Lake County stop him on that run."

Sure enough, the attempt was successful and the Martin drive continued. Shanklin scored from 42 yards out, and the Martin defense held Lake County on their next series. Another drive ended with a Bragg touchdown, and Martin took the lead 21-20.

Lake County was far from ready to surrender, however, and proceeded to march down the field to score, taking a 26-21 lead with a little over 2:00 minutes left in the game. Under pressure, the Martin offense produced one more time, with Johnny Shanklin taking the ball 27 yards for the score and a 27-26 lead.

Lake County got the ball with a few seconds remaining and made a valiant attempt to go downfield. In a dramatic conclusion, Bobby Morrison – he of the recently-repentant attitude toward the Lord – intercepted the pass and the victory was sealed.

6-0 never tasted so sweet!

The final four games of the regular season went to Martin in fairly convincing fashion. The victories came over Obion County Central, Alamo, Greenfield, and – in an especially significant game for the seniors – over Dresden (the last team to have beaten them) by a score of 48-0 to finish the year.

All that remained was a game to determine the champion of the Reelfoot Athletic Conference. That game was the Jaycee Bowl in Milan, Tennessee. The opponent: the Lake County Falcons.

The rematch was highly anticipated, to say the least. Coach Jim Graves remembers that, the week before the game, he was scheduled to appear on the radio program, "The Coaches' Corner," sponsored by station WCMT in Martin. The Lake County coach was also to be in attendance, and had been quoted in the newspaper that week as saying, "Well, I'll tell you one thing: Martin better buckle their chinstraps when they come to play us in Milan!"

Coach Graves recounted the Saturday morning encounter this way:

"I came in and sat down, acknowledging the host and the opposing coach – who was actually my good friend. As the show got underway, I got up from my seat and started toward the door, prompting the host to ask, 'Coach, where are you going?' I responded to him, 'Oh, I forgot my chinstrap out in my car; I was just going to get it.'"

The message was delivered; so was the victory.

The Panthers never allowed the Falcons to make the game close. The final score was 38-20 with senior fullback Richard Bragg rushing for 157 yards and three touchdowns – one of which came on a 90-yard kickoff return on a "trick" double handoff. Mike Beeler, Mickey McAdoo, and Bobby Morrison rounded out the Panther scoring attack. Bragg would later earn All-State honors for his accomplishments.

The season was complete; the record was perfect. Hundreds of Martin fans basked in the glow of the football team's success. Yet, an incident after the season was a reminder that all was not yet well in the world of race relations and sports.

Coach Graves also served as the school's track coach, and on the way home from an away track meet, had his team's bus pull over at a local restaurant, so that the guys could grab a quick meal. They checked in with the owner to be sure he could accommodate the team, which he assured them he could. As the athletes filed in, Johnny Shanklin and L.C. Windom – two black players on the team – came along.

The store owner spoke to Coach Graves and said, "I'm sorry; I can't serve them."

Coach Graves asked, "You can't serve who?"

"I can't serve your niggers. We don't do that here. The rest of your boys are welcome to eat, but they'll have to wait outside."

Coach Graves looked around, then called out to his team: "Come on, fellas, we're getting back on the bus. Looks like we'll be eating somewhere else tonight."

For reasons known only to the coach, and perhaps a handful of others, 1967 was Jim Graves' final season at the helm of the Martin Panthers. He had laid a solid foundation for football at the school and many of his players would form the nucleus for the great things yet to come.

His involvement with the winning streak was not over, though; Jim Graves would return to Martin and play a significant role yet again.

But, that's a story for another chapter.

Chapter Two: Transition

The success of the undefeated season lasted through the following spring, when players come out for drills and coaches look for new talent in order to replace departing players. Literally, every season brings a new team, even if there is a solid core of veteran players returning.

Don Jacobs, whose family had recently returned to Martin from Lansing, Michigan, did not play football his freshman year. As spring practice was commencing, Jacobs said that he ran into Coach Graves in the hallway, and the coach said, "Jacobs – you need to go down to the weight room instead of wandering around up here. And you need to come play football for us."

Don (known affectionately as "Duck" by his teammates) said, "I didn't have anything else to do – so I went!"

Other players prepared to move up the depth chart, and the buzz around the new season which would commence in the fall was palpable.

Then, things changed…

Coach Graves – who had built the Martin program into a powerhouse – announced at the end of the year that he was leaving coaching, and would be accepting a position at the University of Tennessee at Martin (UTM.)

To say that the team, the school, and the community were shocked would be the understatement of the decade, if not the century. There were multiple pleas with the coach, with the school's administration, and perhaps even with the Almighty to get the decision reversed. But Graves remained firm – and the leadership of the Martin football program was up in the air.

Where would they turn for a coach to guide the continued success of the program? Could anyone fill the shoes of the highly-respected Jim Graves?

As it turned out, the solution was close at hand, in the form of another Jim.

Coach James "Jimmy" Dunn had labored for several years on the junior high level – and assembled a modest little streak of his own. With many of the players that would now form the core of the Panther team for 1968, Coach Dunn had led Martin Junior High to two undefeated seasons (a combined 10-0 record.) Martin High

School principal Mac Buckley made the call, and Martin had a new coach.

David Byars, a fresh graduate from UTM and former star player himself at Martin High School, was tapped as Dunn's assistant. No one – including the coaches themselves – was really sure what would happen when the team reported for fall practice. They certainly had no idea whether the success the Panther program had become accustomed to would continue.

But, in the manner that his players would later come to characterize as calm and steadying, Coach Dunn called his first team together and said, "Let's get to work, boys. Why don't you give me five laps?"

As much as anything, that workmanlike attitude would permeate the 1968 season. Conditioning was a key aspect for Coach Dunn, as well as thorough review of the fundamentals. Inheriting a team full of talent and an offensive system that worked, Dunn was wise enough to know that he didn't have to reinvent the wheel.

Turning the offensive reins over to Byars, Dunn worked to solidify the Panther defense. Kenny Winstead, a defensive back, remembers the intensity of the practices.

"We were working on our goal line defense one practice, and Coach Dunn had me, Bobby Morrison, and Johnny Shanklin running a particular play at big Joe Martin."

Joe was a stalwart defensive tackle, playing at 6 feet, 7 inches tall and weighing 260 pounds. By the standards of the time, he really was BIG Joe. (As a matter of fact, for several years afterward, Joe's size 19 football cleats were on display in the trophy case at Westview High School – sort of like retiring his jersey, one might suppose!)

Winstead continues: "Coach Dunn said, 'You have to block him, Winstead; Morrison will help you with the double team.' So we ran the play, and sure enough we were somehow able to block Joe. Coach Dunn blew the whistle and jumped all over the big man, then told us to run it again. We ran it again, and we blocked him again. 'Do it over!' Dunn shouted. So, for the third time, I ran in and blocked Joe, this time with the assistance of Johnny Shanklin."

The coach and his star defensive player were both pretty worked up by this point, but Dunn finally had Martin right where he wanted him, apparently.

Kenny finishes the story:

"When we ran the play for the fourth time, Joe took his right knee and smashed me in the helmet. I crumpled like a rag doll. He tossed Shanklin aside and went after Bobby, and tore him up pretty good.

Everybody in the place went wild. We knew we had something special in Joe Martin."

Martin wasn't the only thing special about the Panther defense as the season opened. Union City couldn't score as the first victory of the Dunn era was posted 28-0. The next week, a similar result had the Panthers victorious over Obion County Central 34-0.

Wins 3, 4, and 5 that season saw the defense give up a total of only 19 points, mostly late in the games when the second and third teams were playing. South Fulton went down 64-6; Gleason was subdued 39-6; and Sharon felt the rumble of the Panthers to the tune of 51-7.

Like the unbeaten season a year earlier, the offense was led by the dominant combination of Bobby Morrison and Johnny Shanklin. The duo was practically unstoppable, especially when assisted by Martin's "new" twist in the backfield, Gene Leonard.

The stat sheet was impressive in the 5-0 run to open the 1968 season. Martin scored 216 points, while holding their opponents to 19.

It appeared the transition under Jimmy Dunn was going well. The question people began to ask was, was there any team that would be able to give the Panthers a real challenge?

The answer to that question came the very next week, as Martin traveled to Trenton to do battle with the Peabody Golden Tide.

42-0

Chapter Three: The Streak Begins

October 11, 1968 was the date that "The Streak" was born, you might say.

Though Martin High had won all of its games in 1967, and was now undefeated halfway through the 1968 season, no one had actively called their success a winning streak. Maybe the coaches were afraid of the jinx – Dunn was as much a "one-game-at-a-time" man as Bear Bryant or any of the other coaching legends of the time.

Players don't remember talking about it, either; the news media was showing a growing interest in the Panther program, but still – no one had yet envisioned a streak.

On this crisp fall evening, Coach Walter Kilzer had his Trenton team poised and ready for the mighty Panthers. Taking the opening kickoff, the Tide rolled 80 yards downfield on a drive that sent a signal to the vaunted Panther defense. "We know you're good, but we're here to play!"

Martin got the ball, and proceeded to score on a lengthy drive of its own – with Leonard, Morrison, and Shanklin alternating runs. Shanklin scored on a final 23-yard run, but Martin missed on the extra point. The Panthers trailed for the first time all season.

The night would see the teams trade defensive stops and touchdowns, with the score tied 13-13 at the half, and 19-19 at the end of the third quarter.

As the fourth quarter began, it was the Martin defense that rose up and made the difference in the game. Two fumbles by Shanklin and Morrison – uncharacteristic of the dynamic duo – gave Trenton its chances to go ahead. But, both drives were thwarted by the Panther defense.

A final opportunity for Trenton came late in the fourth quarter, as the Tide drove for a first down on the Martin 27 yard line. A quarterback sack resulted in a 10-yard loss, followed by Trenton recovering 9 of those yards back on two runs. Finally, on fourth and 11, Trenton gained 8 yards – stopped by Dunn's defense three yards short at the 20.

From there, it was up to the suddenly-jittery Panther offense.

Alternating Leonard (who gained 43 very tough but important yards on the night), Morrison (who picked up 94 yards for his contribution), and Shanklin (whose total was an impressive 240 yards) – the Panthers marched one more time deep into Trenton territory. With 1:40 left on the clock, it was Johnny Shanklin scoring his fourth touchdown of the night from the 8-yard line, putting the Panthers up 25-19.

The Martin defense allowed Trenton to cross midfield, but that was as far as they went before time expired. In their first real test of the season, the Panthers overcame errors and a determined opponent and did what all good teams must do sooner or later.

They found a way to win.

Ed M. Chenette, the sports editor for the *Weakley County Press*, was the first person to write the actual words, now calling Martin's string of 17 consecutive victories a "winning streak." That term, and all that it came to symbolize for the team and the community, would face many challenges in the games and seasons that lay ahead.

But on this night, it was a victory hard-fought and well-earned.

For all of the attention centered on the football field in 1968, it is hard to ignore the fact that this was a most extraordinary year in American history as well.

In April, Dr. Martin Luther King, Jr., was shot and killed on the balcony of the Lorraine Motel in Memphis, TN. The National Guard, including members of the Martin, TN unit, was deployed in

Memphis to help "keep the peace." The shooter was alleged to be James Earl Ray, who later confessed and received a life sentence in prison.

In June, Senator Robert F. Kennedy was shot and killed while campaigning for President in California. The accused shooter, Sirhan B. Sirhan, originally pled not guilty, but was convicted and sentenced to death. (The sentence was later commuted to life in prison.)

The summer produced some hot politics as George W. Wallace of Alabama, running on a strong segregationist platform, ran a surprisingly effective race as an independent candidate. (Eventually, Richard M. Nixon was nominated by the Republicans, and Hubert H. Humphrey by the Democrats.)

The Democratic Convention in Chicago was characterized by violence, protests, tough (some would say brutal) police actions, and unrest over racial and Vietnam war issues.

The Soviet Union invaded (and brutally overran) Czechoslovakia, further upping the tensions in the "Cold War" with the US.

Richard M. Nixon was elected President in November.

With trouble on the news every night, life in Martin proceeded in a relatively peaceful manner. Race relations and strident politics seemed a long ways away on Friday nights under the lights.

Church life was significant for many of the teenagers and their families. The local Church of Christ had a strong program for high schoolers, and the First Baptist Church sponsored what became a local, as well as national, youth event in 1968: *Good News*, A Christian Folk Musical.

Phil Dane remembers, "That Good News choir was so important to me that I thought about quitting the football team so that I could go on the summer choir tour. The coach would have given me time off, but I would have had to run about 14 days' worth of grass drills.

"My friend and teammate, Terry Brockwell, came to my house and told me, 'Phil, you can't quit, man! I know the choir needs you, but we need you, too! You've got to do what you've got to do!'

"I decided I couldn't give up on my teammates, since they weren't giving up on me. I did go on the choir tour – and I ran my grass drills when I got back home. And I'm glad I did.

"But that's just an illustration of what it was like for us on the team. When you know you've got your teammates pulling for you, you feel like you can accomplish anything."

No doubt the team was pulling together, and things were going their way. But, every season has its challenges and adversities that must be overcome. The Panthers weren't through having to pull with and for each other.

Next up – a trip down to Tiptonville and the always-tough Lake County team.

Chapter Four: Cogs in the Machine

As the season turned toward its ending, it became apparent that the Martin football machine was on the verge of becoming dominant. Most great teams – and memorable records – are built around either a great player or two (think Michael Jordan or Joe Montana) or around a great coach (think John Wooden or Vince Lombardi.)

In the case of the Panthers, however, it is both unfair and quite simply impossible to single out one player – or coach, for that matter – as the absolute key to success.

It really was about teamwork.

With the test at Trenton behind them, the Panthers next had to take on one of their perennial rivals – the Falcons of Lake County. With more than 750 fans in attendance in Tiptonville – which was a large crowd at the time – the Martin machine went into methodical gear, handing the ball to Morrison, Shanklin, and Leonard in rugged rotation.

Smoothly and efficiently running the offense was sophomore quarterback Danny Walker – himself a strong runner, but most of all an apt student of the game. His calls and execution kept the Lake County defenders off balance all night, and the balance of the attack is borne out in the final stats: Morrison had 3 touchdowns and 143 yards, while Shanklin added 2 touchdowns and 126 yards. Each back had 20 carries, while Leonard rounded out the action with 71 yards on 14 carries. The Martin ground game was punishing and relentless.

The defense continued its stifling ways, as well. Four different players intercepted Lake County passes: Don Jacobs, Bobby Morrison, Terry Crowe, and Cary Henson. The final score was 31-21, one of those games that seemed closer than it actually was at the end.

At Alamo the following week, Martin again went primarily to the ground game and "ground" up the Red Devils 25-0. The starters played only the first half, with significant substitutes Keith Stover and Ronnie Shanklin getting a chance to showcase Martin's future. Barry Buckley, another young Panther player soon to step up on defense, recovered an Alamo fumble to thwart a scoring drive in the third quarter.

A scary moment for the Panther faithful came when it was discovered that Bobby Morrison was injured, and would not be able to play against division rival Greenfield the following week. Would the ground game continue to be effective without its star tailback?

Johnny Shanklin remembers that, before the game, Morrison called him over to the bench, where Bobby was standing on crutches. "Shank, I can't get out there tonight; you're gonna need to step it up. It's all up to you, Shank; it's all up to you!"

42-0

Shanklin concluded, "I was so young and naïve, I believed him!"

Moving from fullback to tailback, all Shanklin produced that night was 5 touchdowns and 301 yards rushing. Gene Leonard got another score, and again, young Keith Stover filled in at fullback with impressive results.

All of the Martin players were efficient cogs in the machine that was moving toward another unbeaten season. The final score against Greenfield was 38-13.

One game remained in the regular season – this one against an always bitter foe: the Dresden Lions. Though Dresden never managed to score, their defense kept things close and made the Martin home crowd more than a little nervous. The score stood 6-0 at the half, and only 12-0 at the end of the third quarter. Two plays by quarterback Danny Walker finally broke the game open.

In another preview of things to come, Walker uncorked a 21-yard pass to Stan Betts for a touchdown. Scoring through the air was a relatively new development for the Panthers. Next, Walker put on a running exhibition of his own, going 16 yards for a fourth-quarter score that finally gave some breathing room for the anxious fans. Johnny Shanklin tacked on a 30-yarder for good measure, and the final count of 25-0 was not indicative of just how hard-fought the game really was.

10-0 for the season; yet, one more opportunity remained.

The Reelfoot Conference championship was to be played in Milan against Western Division champ Dyer County. The Choctaws were spoiling to put an end to the Martin "streak," as tempers flared a little high during pre-game warmups.

Since Johnny Shanklin had filled in so admirably for the injured Bobby Morrison in the two previous games, the Dyer County team had practiced some special formations designed to stop Shanklin. One of their players, an all-conference linebacker, was overheard to say, "We're gonna stop your nigger tonight!"

Danny Walker remembers telling his coach, "I'm afraid we're going to have some trouble out of that guy."

No problem. The quick-thinking Dunn outlined a strategy which the Panthers employed on their first series. It involved a play known as an "isolation" block.

In an isolation play, a key player on the opposing side is identified and targeted with two blockers, who arrive just ahead of the running back who is carrying the ball. Of course, in this case, the opposing player was the loud-mouthed linebacker.

Dunn said, "Run the play; then run it again; then run it again."

That's exactly what the Panthers did, sending blocker after blocker directly at the unsuspecting player. Each time, the ball was handed off to Shanklin. The result was a merciless pounding that sent the player to the sidelines and eventually, out of the game -- and a Shanklin touchdown to set off the Martin scoring.

Much to the surprise of both the Martin fans and the Dyer County defense, Bobby Morrison stepped back on to the field and into his tailback spot in the offense. As some football pundits have proclaimed at similar times, it was all over but the slow walk and the crying. Morrison ripped the Dyer County defense for two more touchdowns, and the game was all but over.

Martin's stalwart defense did the rest, allowing only a late touchdown that mattered very little. The score was 20-7, and the Martin Panthers were conference champions – and undefeated – for the second year in a row.

The Jimmy Dunn era was off to a perfect start, and the streak now stood at 22-0.

Excitement abounded, but so did some serious questions. With the graduation of Morrison and Shanklin, as well as some of the team's most experienced linemen and defensive players – just how good could the Panthers of 1969 possibly be?

Chapter Five: Growth and Change

1969 was one heck of a year – everywhere.

Richard Nixon began his first term as President of the United States, and set about dealing with the very unpopular Vietnam War. The world was transfixed as live television broadcast the first humans to land on the Moon – Neil Armstrong, Buzz Aldrin, with Michael Collins orbiting above in Apollo 11.

One of the most emblematic moments in the youth-oriented counterculture movement arrived that summer in a field outside of Woodstock, New York – with the likes of Janis Joplin, Joan Baez, Jimi Hendrix, The Who, and the Grateful Dead imploring the world for peace, love, and rock and roll.

Finally, two other forces that would shape young minds for years to come debuted in 1969: the show by the Children's Television Network, known as *Sesame Street*; and a military defense network of computers originally named ARPA Net – which became the backbone for what we now commonly call the Internet.

Change and growth were the order of the day in Martin, Tennessee, as well. With the upgrading and expansion of the University of Tennessee system, the Martin campus was changing from a "branch" of the state university to a full-fledged, four-year school. Many new faculty members and staff moved to the area, bringing their families with them.

It was a good time for local business and industry, as well. Companies like Miller Lighting, previously headquartered in Ohio, made the move to Martin as economic factors and a warmer climate were strong inducements. Again, this brought new families to the area and added to the school rolls at all levels.

For the Panther football team, a significant new addition was Mark Stafford, a strapping athlete who had played a number of sports in Ohio. Mark remembers being intrigued by the move with his family, though to him, Martin was a relatively big place.

"Yes, I actually got lost in Martin, Tennessee not long after we moved here," Stafford confessed with a laugh. "My town was pretty small."

Stafford had always played tackle in high school, but the Martin line was pretty well stocked coming into the '69 season. Coaches Dunn and Byars asked him if he had ever thought about playing tight end. "I'd never caught a football, but I told them I'd sure be willing to try," Stafford responded.

42-0

That decision became part of an explosive new dimension for the 1969 Panther team.

Danny Walker had shown some promise in throwing the football a season earlier, but with the potent Panther ground attack hitting on all cylinders, the passing game had remained something of a novelty in the offense. Now, with veteran running backs Johnny Shanklin, Bobby Morrison, and Gene Leonard all graduated, no one was quite sure what the offense would be able to produce.

Not that the Panthers were hopeless in the backfield. Junior Keith Stover had gained valuable experience in the previous season, filling in for the injured Morrison. Johnny Shanklin's younger brother, Ronnie, was now ready to step up and take his turn in the backfield. Cary Henson rounded out the new Martin back attack -- along with Walker at quarterback – but all eyes were soon looking downfield as a set of brand new weapons were revealed.

The opening game was against set against the Union City Golden Tornado, now being led by former Martin High coach James Graves, who had returned to coaching after spending a year at the University of Tennessee.

The verdict was delivered fairly quickly as the Panthers opened a 22-6 lead in the first quarter, capped by a 55-yard touchdown pass from Danny Walker to Mark Stafford. Ricky Perry and Keith Stover had rushing touchdowns, and one more touchdown pass from Walker to Stafford rounded out the scoring.

The Panthers showed that a potent defense was going to be characteristic of the team again, as linebacker Joey Taylor led a stingy group that held Union City to -4 yards of total offense for the first half and 12 basically inconsequential points for the game.

By the second game of the season, versus Obion County Central, another passing threat emerged in the person of Rick Wilson, who played the end opposite Mark Stafford. Danny Walker found Wilson for one touchdown and threw two more to Stafford; Ronnie Shanklin scored his first rushing touchdown, answering many questions about his ability to succeed his brother.

(There would be lots of highlights yet to come in the younger Shanklin's stellar career.)

The second team saw considerable action as the final tally was Martin 39, Obion Central 6. The streak was now at 24 games.

Up next was a visit by South Fulton; the Red Devils were outmanned and outgunned, as the ever-growing passing attack produced two more Walker-to-Stafford touchdowns, 3 rushing touchdowns by Stover and Shanklin (who had 2), and a special-teams score on a 56-yard punt return by Cary Henson. Martin 41, South Fulton 14.

Gleason fell to Martin 30-0 in the fourth victory of the season; Stover and Shanklin each scored two touchdowns. Suddenly, the news broke that Martin was within a game of tying a long-standing state record for consecutive victories – reported as 27 wins in a row by Kingsport Dobyns-Bennett High School 20 years earlier.

There was, of course, a great deal of interest and emotion as Martin traveled the short 7 miles down the road to neighboring Sharon, Tennessee for an attempt at the record versus the Eagles. Though starting slowly, the Panther juggernaut was not to be denied as the final score mounted to 41-0. A headline in the Memphis *Commercial-Appeal* newspaper touted the "record 27th consecutive victory."

The following week, Martin had a complete game performance against Trenton to record their 28th consecutive win (and what they thought was a new state record) – 46-21. The ground attack tallied six touchdowns, and Walker threw to Wilson for one more.

Jubilation ensued as a vocal convoy of fans decorated cars, honked horns, and celebrated all the way home. A new state record belonged to Martin.

Alas, it seemed that the celebration was a bit premature; after some double-checking, the Tennessee Secondary Schools Athletic Association (TSSAA), the governing agency for high school sports in the state, found that an error in recording the victories for Kingsport had resulted in the notice of 27 consecutive games "without a defeat." It was actually 37 games, with one of the games in question possibly being a tie.

The Panthers were momentarily disappointed, but as Rick Wilson remembers, the mood in the locker room was, "Well, we just have to win 10 more!"

As had happened already twice before, the road to the record ran perilously through the team from Lake County, which was up next, primed for one more shot at upsetting Martin's record-breaking plans.

Playing on the home field in Martin, the Panthers came out slow and listless. Perhaps it was the news about the record being pulled out from under them; maybe it was the pressure of the streak itself, beginning to grow.

Whatever the reason, Martin trailed the Falcons at the half, by a score of 8-0.

Senior center and team captain Walter Benson remembers, "We were definitely sluggish in that first half. But Coach Dunn came in and lit a fire under our ass at halftime, and things picked up pretty quick."

Others remember that a student teacher and UTM football player – Don Delfino – might have added a word or two to the "ass firing" that Walter recounts.

In front of what was estimated to be a crowd approaching 6,000 people – "one of the largest crowds ever to attend a high school football game in Martin," per the *Weakley County Press* – defensive end Bubba Dodd led a surge of pressure that jangled the Lake County offense and generated opportunities for the Martin offense. Dodd finished the night with 15 unassisted tackles, several of them behind the line of scrimmage.

The Martin ground game woke up and Cary Henson carried for two touchdowns, with Keith Stover adding a final score for a 21-8 margin.

The next week, against Alamo, the Panthers of old seemed to have returned, as Martin ground up the Red Devils 35-6. Ronnie Shanklin had a breakout performance with 3 touchdowns and over 150 yards rushing. Keith Stover and Barry Simpson each added TD's, as well.

The defense was stifling, technically pitching another shutout. The Alamo score came on a 56-yard return of a fumble by the Martin offense with less than a minute remaining in the game.

Martin was now the 13th-ranked team in Tennessee, at a time when all schools were ranked together (before the current classification into smaller and larger schools was put into place.)

The streak stood at 30 games.

An anticipated duel with long-time foe Greenfield turned out not to be much of a fight, as the Panther rushing attack produced 360 yards for the game, spreading touchdowns among Cary Henson (who had two), Ronnie Shanklin, Danny Walker, and Ricky Perry. Greenfield scored once in the first quarter, and once in the last quarter to make the final count 33-14.

Nine wins for the year; streak extended to 31 in a row. Now, all that stood between Martin and an almost unheard-of third undefeated season was their old nemesis, the Dresden Lions. Many remembered – on both the Martin and Dresden sidelines – that Dresden was the last team to tame the mighty Panthers in the final game of 1966, by a score of 7-6.

Ed Chenette, writing for the *Weakley County Press* in advance of the game, wrote:

> Can Dresden pull of what would have to be the BIG BIG UPSET of the year? One of the largest crowds in Dresden history will be on hand, and more than a smattering of them

will be Panther fans. We hope the weather will cooperate and make the game a true test of both teams.

It is doubtful that Mr. Chenette knew just how ominous his words would prove to be on the following Friday night.

John Fairless

Chapter 6: Cold's Not the Word for It

It can get pretty cold in mid-November in Northwest Tennessee, especially after the sun goes down early in the evening. On November 14, 1969, the temperature on the field in Dresden at game time was 12° F. Snow flurries had been drifting down all throughout the day, and the ground was crusted with ice. There was some question as to whether the game would be played that night, but the determination was made to play – so the stadium filled and the teams got ready.

It was, indeed, a capacity crowd; hundreds of fans made the drive from Martin, and Dresden's turnout filled their bleachers. The main objective early on was to stay warm! There were fires burning in barrels all around the field, and fans huddled close together under blankets and heavy coats.

Through a quirk of events, the Martin players ended up with nowhere to get dressed for the game; Dresden did not have a visitor's locker room (part of the psychological game for opposing teams?) – and, though normally the Panthers could have dressed in their own locker room and ridden the bus over to the Dresden field, the weather had knocked out the electricity in Martin and there were no lights or heat there.

So, the team improvised. Managers and a few parents helped out, holding flashlights outside the team bus while the boys unloaded and began putting on their equipment. Because of the cold, there were lots of extra pads, long-sleeve shirts, and other items put on in addition to the normal uniforms.

Kenny Winstead remembers, "I had on so many pads and extra layers, I felt like the Mummy. I could barely move."

Warm-ups took on a whole new meaning as the teams took the field in the pre-game ritual to prepare. There was some talking back and forth, and a few bumps and shoves before the game even got started. "It's all part of the game," Winstead said. "Both sides were ready to go at it."

It appeared that Martin might open the game up like any other, scoring twice in the first quarter to take a 12-0 lead. The fans were happy, especially after Dresden fumbled a punt at their own 4-yard line and the Panthers recovered. Keith Stover took the next play into the end zone for a quick touchdown.

Next, it was Cary Henson ripping off a 55-yard run for the second TD of the night. If there were any thoughts of a blowout or an easy victory in the making, those ideas were quickly dispelled.

Dresden took over after the Martin kickoff and drove the ball 80 yards for a score; a two-point conversion made it 12-8 at the end of the first quarter. The second quarter proved to be a bit of a defensive

42-0

tussle, with both teams trading stops and punts. In fact, it was a punt play just before the second half that shocked the crowd and added to the drama of the night – and became a story that is still told, by the Martin faithful, at least – to this day.

The Dresden defense had become stingy after Martin's opening scores, and had the Panthers backed up in their own territory late in the half. After Ronnie Shanklin was stopped twice for no gain, and Cary Henson could manage only two yards, the Panthers were forced to punt. Rick Wilson got off a good kick, out to the Panther 40-yard line. The kick was fielded by Dresden's Crawford, who immediately lateraled (tossed the ball backwards to his own player) to Johnson.

What happened next is a matter of great dispute.

According to the Martin players, a whistle sounded from the Dresden sideline – the sound that every player is taught means, "Stop the play!" All of the Martin players immediately ceased running, and made no effort to tackle the Dresden runner.

The Dresden players had other ideas, however, and kept the play going – for 40 yards into the end zone. The referees signaled that it was a touchdown. The Martin players began protesting, claiming that they had heard a whistle. A quick conference of the officials produced the decision that none of them had blown it, therefore the play was good.

To say that a "heated" discussion took place next would be an understatement. Coaches and fans charged out onto the field. J.C. Henson – the father of Panther running back Cary Henson and Athletic Director at UT Martin – approached the head official and demanded that the play be called back. "They blew a whistle!" Coach Henson shouted.

As a result of his impassioned plea, Mr. Henson was escorted back to the sideline and instructed not to set foot on the field again, or he would be ejected from the stadium. The officials refused to budge, and the score stood 14-12 in favor of Dresden at the half.

Walter Benson remembers that the discussions in the Martin huddle – over behind the buses – was pretty fiery, as well. The team was mad about the call, but more frustrated with themselves for not playing like the champions they felt they were. Pads and extra layers of clothing were ripped off, and his instructions to the team heading back out to the field were, "Let's go play like we know we can play!"

That meant a steady dose of the potent Panther backfield, and a reignited defensive unit that was bound and determined not to get beat by trickery. The result was 3 second-half touchdowns by Ronnie Shanklin and a complete shutdown of the Dresden offensive unit. The final score was Martin 32, Dresden 12.

Emotions were high, and when the game was over, things weren't quite over. Dresden's field was comparatively small and the fans from both sides were in tight quarters. With so much activity on the field during the game, it was probably bound to spill over off the field, as well. Fistfights broke out, and as the Martin team huddled in the end zone for its traditional post-game prayer, fans from Dresden circled them and began to shout. According to several players, they were not delivering congratulations or encouraging words.

Randy Brundige, a senior on the team that year, remembers one man in particular who began cursing the Martin team; as his volume increased, so did the string of profanity he was using. Some of the Martin parents had arrived by this time and began to insist that the man leave the team alone. He would hear none of it.

Finally, Randy's father, H.C. Brundige, who was Martin's mayor at the time, reached out to subdue the gentleman. There was something of a scuffle, and Randy's younger cousin, Johnny Brundige, said, "All I remember was looking up after the prayer and seeing Uncle Ham with his arms around some guy's neck, dragging him off the field."

Sometimes, you just have to stick up for your own.

Finally, the emotions cooled and the crowd began to disperse. But one more piece of business remained for the now undefeated Panthers, whose record stood at 10-0. The streak, of course, was now 32 consecutive wins.

In the days before the state playoff system, being invited to a bowl game after the season was not automatic, and the matchups were sometimes unpredictable. There was no longer a playoff for the Reelfoot Conference championship as there had been in the two previous seasons, so the Panthers had to decide whether or not they would accept a bowl bid, if one was offered.

Of course, the 32-game streak was a prize that lots of other teams wanted to capture – especially some of the bigger schools in areas like Jackson or Brownsville. There was talk that Martin's streak was "cheap" and came at the expense of smaller schools.

Coach Dunn put the question to his seniors after that game that night: "Should we accept a bid to a bowl game against a larger school, if they offer it to us? Or should we wait and play again next season to try and extend the streak?"

It was a gut-wrenching choice, either way; not every player on the squad felt the same way, but all got to have their say. Some were ready to play on, and take on any comer. Others saw the wisdom in preserving the streak, and felt that a bowl matchup might be a "set-up" designed to end Martin's dominance.

In the end, Walter Benson remembers that the seniors handed it over to the strong class of juniors who would be leading the 1970 team.

The decision would be theirs. The team would support whichever choice was made.

So, there was no bowl game in 1969. Martin would live to play another day, and the streak would continue for one season more.

In a salute to the football team sponsored by the Martin Methodist Men's Organization after the season, Tennessee-Martin head football coach Robert Carroll had these words for the team:

> You young men and your coaches should be proud of 32 consecutive victories; I can assure you that every citizen of Martin takes pride in your accomplishments. Football is now in its 100th year and I can assure you that very, very few teams on any level have ever achieved what you have….
>
> Remember, that in football and in life, you should use your God-given talents to the best of your abilities. That is what makes you a winner.

With the tumultuous decade of the 1960's ending – and with hopes rising for better times ahead – perhaps it was a genuine sign of the times that the year's top-selling song was the feel-good, one-hit wonder *Sugar, Sugar* by a band known as **The Archies**. Coming in just after that was **The Fifth Dimension** with *The Age of Aquarius*, something of a mysterious sound that asked questions and shared visions about that same future.

Certainly, change was in the air and a new team would take over the reins of the streak. Three seasons in a row – would there be four?

Chapter 7: The Path for a Champion

The 1969 Panther football team – of Martin High School – was to be the last that ever played a game. With a new year and a new decade dawning, 1970 saw the consolidation of two schools in the Weakley County School System: Martin High and Sharon High were merged, resulting in the freshly-minted Westview High School. The team nickname, chosen from submissions from students of both schools, was to be the Chargers.

As far as the two communities were concerned, there was a bit of unrest over the "new-fangled idea" of consolidation. Budgetary considerations spoke in favor of the smaller Sharon school aligning with the larger student body in Martin; geographically, the two towns were closer together than any other two municipalities in the county, so transportation was also deemed to be beneficial. With larger class sizes, it was reasoned, more state money would be available to offer an enhanced curriculum including advanced subjects and foreign languages.

But, community spirit – so often embodied in the local sports teams – runs deep, and it was a bit unsettling for both towns to "give up" their school and their team. Initially, no one felt like they were gaining anything. Rather, both student bodies felt a bit adrift.

But, that first senior class of Westview High School was a spirited bunch, and everybody showed up and decided to give it a good effort. (The new school's facilities were not finished by opening day, and Sharon students were bussed over to Martin to attend class in the old Martin High building.)

One of the great questions, of course, involved the winning streak that the Martin football teams had built over the previous three seasons. Would the streak now pass to Westview? Would a new record have to begin, giving Martin an admirable, but now-defunct standard of 32 wins in a row? Though Westview was 0-0 to start the season, just like everybody else, were they still playing to extend the streak and go for a state record?

The governing body for high school sports was the Tennessee Secondary Schools Athletic Association – the TSSAA. Over the summer, that group met and decided that, since the Martin program was, indeed, passing intact to the new Westview school, the win streak should be allowed to continue, even with the addition of players from Sharon.

Of course, the 10 other teams on the schedule for the 1970 season had high hopes of bringing that streak to an end. None was more primed to do so than the Golden Tornado of Union City, under the watchful eye of former Martin coach Jim Graves. The Chargers were on the road for the season opener.

42-0

Opening night dawned crisp and clear – well, not exactly clear, as the skies opened up about midway through the first half of the game and began to rain quite heavily. The Chargers had been outfitted with brand new football shoes – cleats, as they were commonly known – and the team members were excited about the color: white. It was a bold and daring look, befitting the new "cool" decade of the 70's and the championship vibe that this team felt.

There was only one problem; the cleats were designed for soccer, and not necessarily for down-and-dirty, get-in-the-trenches football. As field conditions worsened with the rain, Phil Dane remembers, "the white cleats looked great, but the spikes were ½-inch, instead of the ¾-inch we were used to. And they had these rounded tips, so that when the field got wet, nobody could stand up."

Rain or no, what mattered to the Westview faithful was that, deep in the fourth quarter, their team was down 15-8, and they could see the streak and the record slipping away. So, they did what would become a hallmark of the team in a number of close games that season – they fought their way through to the end.

Ronnie Shanklin, picking up where he had left off the season before, pounded the Union City defense for three touchdowns and two two-point conversions. After Shanklin's final TD put the Chargers ahead, Danny Walker and Mark Stafford sealed the deal with another two-point conversion on the pass. The final score was 24-21, Westview on top for consecutive victory number 33.

Again, *Weakley County Press* sports editor, Ed Chenette, said it so eloquently:

> A lesser team might have panicked after UC got a 'bomb' on the third offensive play of the game when Drerup went 69 yards.
>
> A lesser team might also have become discouraged after being hit time and again with penalties that mounted up to about 120 yard before the game had ended.
>
> And a lesser team might also have folded after losing the ball on a fumble on the UC 10 at a time UC led 15-8 in the fourth period.
>
> But this is not a lesser team, and the Chargers maintained their cool, and continued to plug away.

As for the new, white cleats? They were gone after the game, never to return to the Charger sideline that season.

The following week, the Chargers traveled again, this time deeper into Obion County to take on the Rebels of Obion County Central.

42-0

Befitting their increasing stature, the Chargers were now drawing press coverage from the "big time" papers in Memphis, with that city's *Commercial-Appeal* taking note of the approaching 34th game in the streak. The *Weakley County Press* was proud to announce that the Chargers had been given a ranking as the #5 team in the state.

The Rebels offered little resistance to the Chargers on this night, with the final tally coming in at 37-16, in favor of the Chargers. Mark Stafford and Rick Wilson, the talented ends who made complementary targets for quarterback Danny Walker, accounted for three touchdown receptions. Barry Simpson had a TD reception out of the backfield, as well. Ronnie Shanklin returned an OCC punt for 65 yards and a score, and Johnny Brundige added a field goal.

Next up was the Trenton Peabody Golden Tide – an opponent that had always played Martin tough in the past. Was a similar grudge match in store for Westview in the first home game of the new season and the new era?

The question was seemingly answered in the first 90 seconds of the game, as Westview opened a blitzkrieg of activity that resulted in 22 points before the Tide ever got to run a play. Ronnie Shanklin took the ball 37 yards and a score to conclude the Chargers' opening drive. On the ensuing kickoff, the Tide fumbled and Rick Wilson scooped the ball and scored from 32 yards out. Barry Simpson added a bit of insult to the injury with a 3-yard touchdown run on the next Westview drive, and the rout was on.

Final score: Westview 36, Trenton 0.

Other notable plays from the evening came on a Walker-to-Stafford scoring pass from 15 yards out, and a 4-yard quarterback keeper from Danny Walker for six points. Defensive tackle Robert Starr, one of the additions from the Sharon Eagles team, contributed several wicked hits and picked up two fumble recoveries. Starr was also noted for his size and agility on offense, a "Blind Side" kind of blocker, according to his teammates.

> (*The Blind Side* refers to the book and subsequent movie about the life of Michael Oher, from Memphis, Tennessee. If you happened not to have read it or seen it – you should!)

The following week, Westview was again at home against an in-county foe, the Gleason Bulldogs. Workmanlike in their precision, the Chargers tuned up with 41 points on the board, featuring touchdowns from Keith Stover (5-yard run); two Mark Stafford receptions from Danny Walker (46 yards and 6 yards); a 6-yard run from Ronnie Shanklin and a 2-yard run from Barry Simpson; and a 7-yard TD pass from Walker to Rick Wilson.

Victory # 36 belonged to Westview, 41-16; they were now one game away from tying the state record for consecutive victories – the one that had been clarified in the previous season's fiasco with the TSSAA (ironically, against Sharon High School.)

Kingsport Dobyns-Bennett High School had been undefeated for 37 games in a row from 1946-50; now, 20 years later, Westview hoped finally to equal – and, hopefully, surpass – the mark.

But, there was a BIG obstacle in their path.

The calendar turned to October, and a team of unknown quality but considerable quantity was coming to town. The Bluejays of Charleston, Missouri, ranked #3 in their state and averaging over 206 pounds per player (almost unheard of in those days) would be a stern test for the Chargers.

Coach Jimmy Dunn, master of the understatement, told the Memphis *Commercial-Appeal,* "Well, it's down to this one. You can't say it's just another game."

You can say that again, Coach!

Chapter 8: Destiny Awaits

Back at the start of "the Streak" – in the 1967 season with the Panthers – a good crowd on a Friday night was around 500 fans in attendance. The home field for Westview games – the stadium at the University of Tennessee at Martin – seated about 7,500.

As Coach Dunn noted in his interview with the press before the game, "We've never filled our stadium for a game. The closest was against Lake County last year, when we had between 5,000 and 6,000."

It wasn't quite standing-room-only, but the stadium could have been considered comfortably filled for the Westview-Charleston game on October 9, 1970. The hype was high; Westview would be attempting to tie the Tennessee high school record for consecutive victories in football. The opponent added an element of mystery and intrigue, an out-of-state school with a solid reputation, and a physically intimidating presence, to boot.

Barry Buckley remembers how much the talk was of how Westview was finally going to meet their match. "We were told that they were giants, that there was no way we would be able to play with them." Buckley said that his teammates were determined to present a tough front to the visitors from Missouri; at the pre-game meeting of the captains for the coin toss, "there wasn't any shaking of hands." The game was on, and the Chargers were ready to meet their fate – come what may.

If I may insert just a personal word here – as a 7th-grader that year, I was called up to play in the high school band. This meant that we had reserved seats for every game during the season, and I can remember feeling palpably afraid for our guys.

I had read all the press clippings, and had imagined the Charlestonites to be huge monsters, set on destroying our heroes. In my second season as a player myself (on the junior high football team,) I was sure that much pain was about to be inflicted at the snap of the ball. As I remember it now, that sentiment seemed to be shared by many of us huddling on the Westview sideline.

The whistle blew, the ball was kicked, and the game was on. To say that it was painful would be to completely and utterly fail to describe the carnage that ensued.

The Chargers of Westview scored the first 61 points of the game – all in the first half. The supposedly mighty Charleston team appeared to be in a complete daze, as Shanklin, Stover, Stafford, Walker, Wilson and the rest of the team went over them, around them, and through them as they dropped them to the ground with bone-crunching blocks and tackles.

Phil Dane, Mike Nanney, Johnny Brundige, Tim Prince, and Robert Starr – the supposedly overmatched Westview line (who averaged "only" about 185 pounds)—generally made mincemeat out of the vaunted Charleston behemoths.

It was over – done—finished – kaput—and then, it was halftime.

The reserves mopped up in the second half, and Charleston eventually put 27 points on the board. But all the questions had been answered. The victory belonged to Westview, along with a share of the record in the history books.

The Streak now stood at 37 games.

How fitting that, next up and in line to try to spoil the Charger party, was one of their bitterest rivals and oldest foes. Westview would have to go back on the road for a visit to undefeated Lake County, in quest of victory number 38 and sole possession of the record.

There was absolutely no love lost between the Chargers and the Falcons; as you will recall from earlier chapters, the Martin teams had escaped on more than one occasion by the skin of their teeth, often having to come from behind to defeat Lake County.

On a cold, wet night in Tiptonville, more than 4,000 spectators jammed the field to see history being made – one way or the other.

Westview scored first, on a 4-yard pass from Danny Walker to Rick Wilson; the conversion for two points failed, and the score was 6-0.

Lake County marched down the field next, scoring and kicking the extra point to take a 7-6 lead. Danny Walker calmly led the Charger offense down the field and took the ball himself for a 14-yard score to put the Chargers up 12-7. (PAT's seemed to elude the Chargers on this night.)

The third quarter went the way of the Chargers, and Mark Stafford pulled in a 6-yard touchdown pass from Danny Walker. This time, the try for two was successful on another Walker-to-Stafford hookup, and the Chargers led 20-7. No one on the Westview sideline was breathing easy, however.

Lake County marched back after the kickoff, and broke loose on a 42-yard touchdown run by Haynes, followed with a 2-point conversion by Belk. 20-14, and many in the crowd were thinking, "Oh, boy – here we go again!"

> (Your intrepid band members were wondering just how we were going to escape after the game, unscathed and undamaged.)

42-0

The play of the game – and, perhaps, of the season – occurred with 7:09 to play. The Chargers and Lake had swapped stern defensive stands, and it was time for Westview to punt. Rick Wilson lined up in his own end zone to take the snap, and describes what happened next like this:

> Dane snapped the ball, and as it was settling into my hands, I saw that one of our guys had missed on his blocking assignment. Here came the Lake County player headed straight for me. I didn't know what else to do, as he was clearly going to get to the ball – so I just swung my leg and tried to kick his head off! We both went down, and there was a mad scramble for the ball.

According to the rules of football, if the Lake County player recovered the loose ball in the end zone, the Falcons would be awarded a touchdown – worth 6 points, which would tie the game – and would then have an opportunity to go ahead on the extra point.

If the Chargers recovered the ball in the end zone, Lake County would be credited with a safety – worth 2 points – and would get the ball back after a free kick by Westview. Rick's understated description of a "mad scramble" puts it very mildly, indeed.

As both players struggled to control it, the football squirted out of the end zone, and there was a huddle of the officials to determine who had gained control of the football last.

Again, Wilson remembers:

> The head referee, who just happened to be a TSSAA official from Martin, was speaking very calmly to the group as they all shared what they had seen and what they thought the ruling should be. I heard him say, "Now, fellas – we have a volatile situation here, and we want to be sure to make the right call." I think they were a little worried about their own skins after the game, too.

As it turned out, the ruling was that Wilson had been the last player to control the football, and Lake County was awarded two points and the ball. Wilson had a booming kick to the Lake County 30, but Haynes managed to return it for 36 yards and set up the Falcons' last hurrah at the Westview 34-yard line.

Four plays later, Lake had a first down at the 24; two more plays, and Lake County was at the 19. On third down, the Lake QB was sacked for a one-yard loss, and the final fourth-down heave into the end zone was batted to the ground by Westview's Keath Turner.

Westview took over on downs and ran out the clock to end the game.

The record: 38-0.

42-0

The Chargers had traversed a mountain that no other team had ever climbed.

Once more, we go to Ed Chenette, the faithful sports editor of the *Weakley County Press*, for his summary comment:

> Others, if they wish, may single out this player or that one. But I have no intention of doing that. For this game, the triumph which was the greatest in history, was played and won by every single Charger who appeared on the field. This was a team victory, a victory of defense and offense, and I for one intend to remember it that way.

It was, indeed, a win to remember and a sweet victory to savor – but not for long.

As is the manner of the game, there was another foe to face in just one short week. The Bulldogs of Milan were having a pretty good season of their own, and they were sure to bring out all the stops to try and topple the high-flying Chargers.

Happy to be back in the friendly confines of the UT-Martin stadium, Westview opened the game against Milan in impressive fashion.

Ronnie Shanklin cranked out a 4-yard touchdown run, with Danny Walker tacking on the extra two points, for an 8-0 lead.

Milan came back with a touchdown, but failed to add any extra points; Westview was up 8-6. Keith Stover plunged for a 1-yard touchdown, Walker passed to Stafford for two, and the score was 16-6. An additional Walker-to-Wilson pass made it 22-6 in the third quarter, and the Charger faithful were sitting back in their seats, thankful to be delivered from another barnburner like the Lake County game the previous week.

Ah, but as Shakespeare so succinctly put it, uneasy lies the head that wears the crown!

Milan had another trick or two up its collective sleeve, and the fourth quarter was destined to be a barnburner – and then some! Milan showed some pluck, and went for it on a fourth-down play that turned into a touchdown.

Westview 22-12.

Milan held and Westview was forced to punt; Rick Wilson got off a good kick that would have pinned Milan back in its own end of the field. But, there was a penalty and Wilson had to kick again. This time, Milan's Holmes took it 54 yards to the house and the score was Westview 22, Milan 18 with 2:44 remaining in the game.

42-0

Yogi Berra was famous for saying, "the game ain't over till it's over!" For the Westview football team, Yogi's words were never more true.

Milan tried an onside kick after their score, hoping to get the ball back with one more chance to win. They pulled it off, and had the ball at midfield. The Charger defense bowed its collective neck, though, and Milan was forced into a turnover as Keath Turner intercepted the pass of Milan's Johnny Tucker with 1:22 to go in the game.

Ronnie Shanklin did his best to dig his team out of the hole; a first down would seal the deal and let the clock expire. He appeared to have it at the 16-yard line, but a Charger penalty for the half the distance to the goal put the ball at the 8-yard line. Another penalty on the next play – again for half the distance – and the ball lay on the 4-yard line with less than a minute left to play.

Wilson lined up to punt from his own end zone – and déjà vu was out in full force. The Milan defensive line broke through with a rush, and Rick remembers, "that guy blocked the kick so hard that it bounced off the scoreboard behind my head!"

Two points to Milan; the score is now 22-20 with :19 seconds left.

Westview's Johnny Brundige lined up for the free kick to Milan, and sent the ball sailing to the Milan 25, a kick of nearly 50 yards. Unfortunately for the Charger faithful, Milan's Holmes ran back 36 of those yards and gave the Bulldogs one last shot from the Westview 49, with :04 seconds to go.

Milan went to a "trick play" they had used earlier in the game with great success, a reverse to Holmes from Tucker. This time, the Charger defense sniffed it out and stuffed Mr. Holmes as the game ended.

Number 39 was in the books, and the Charger fans walked weak-kneed away from a victory for the second consecutive week.

In high school football, there was never really such a thing as a "bye week" – an open date on which the team does not play a game – back in those days. But the Chargers got the next best thing, as they traveled to Paris, Tennessee to take on the Henry County Patriots for the chance at win #40.

The final score was Westview 47, Henry County 0. There was lots of scoring to go around, and the second and third teams got to see considerable action. A couple of Westview's starters earned significant distinctions in the game.

42-0

Ronnie Shanklin had been promised by Coach David Byars that, if he rushed for 2,000 yards during his Charger career, he would receive a pair of gold football shoes. (Some say that it was Shanklin who asked the coach for the shoes, though I have not been able to verify Mr. Shanklin's version of the story, as of yet.)

On this night, Ronnie Shanklin eclipsed that mark. True to his word, the coach provided the shoes to Shanklin, who at that point was the career rushing leader for Martin/Westview high schools.

On the defensive side of the ball, Barry "Snake" Buckley played a game for the ages, blocking two Henry County kicks that led to touchdowns for the Chargers, recovering a fumble to end an HCHS drive, and scooping up another fumble for a 25-yard touchdown of his own. Not only that, with Mark Stafford suffering an injury, Buckley subbed in on offense and caught a two-point conversion from Danny Walker after a Charger score.

The story goes that Buckley had been pretty banged up himself after the games of the previous two weeks, and that he had received a little "special" treatment from the Chargers' team physician in preparation for the Henry County game. When asked about it, Snake smiled and said, "Yeah, I was feeling pretty good that night. But that game tape got me a college scholarship." Buckley played collegiately at Harding University in Arkansas.

And so, we come full circle to whence this story began.

The Westview Chargers were now possessors of a 40-game winning streak, a ranking as the #12 team in the state, and were ready to do battle with the only team in West Tennessee more highly regarded than they were.

It was time to meet the undefeated and fifth-ranked Humboldt Rams, in what came to be known simply as, The Game.

Chapter 9: The Game

There was lots going on in the world during 1970: the Vietnam War, highly unpopular amongst many Americans and particularly so with college students, had brought a number of protests across the country. America was shocked when National Guard troops opened fire at Kent State University in Ohio, killing 4 unarmed college students and wounding nine others.

The governments of the world were in a time of uproar: Egypt's leader, Gamal Nasser – a former revolutionary – died and was succeeded by Anwar Sadat, a moderate friendlier to the US.

King Hussein of Jordan ascended to power with a military junta at his side. In popular culture, Jimi Hendrix died of a drug overdose.

Not everything was gloom and doom, however; 1970 saw the debut of *Monday Night Football*, the successful return to Earth of Apollo 13, the first season of television on PBS, and the introduction of the Pinto by the Ford Motor Company.

(On second thought, never mind the Pinto!)

All of this is to say that, outside the confines of rural West Tennessee, there was a wide world and it was busy. But, during the first week of

November 1970, it was all about high school football in this little neck of the woods.

It is impossible to overstate the hype and hyperbole that surrounded a simple high school football game that week. While the communities of Martin and Sharon had begun the year in a somewhat-uneasy, symbiotic relationship that saw the mergers of their two schools, they were now solidly behind the Charger football team and were unified in the desire for a victory over the heavily-favored team from Humboldt.

Local bragging rights can be a pretty fierce thing at the height of a good football rivalry in the South!

The two schools had met once before, 35 years earlier, under similar circumstances; the Rams had been expecting little trouble from the Martin squad then, and seemed to be a bit unconcerned this time around, as well.

(By the way, the 1935 game went Martin's way, 13-12.)

Humboldt's coach, Jim Poteete, had been "overheard" on the Milan radio station a few weeks earlier, giving an interview during halftime of a game. Coach Po was asked what he thought of the prospect of playing Westview in the Jaycee Bowl Game in Milan at the end of the season. His reply: "I'd like to play Westview at 6 o'clock and then meet a really good team at 8:00."

Those comments were posted on bulletin boards, printed in the local paper, and bandied about town feverishly in the run up to the game; the Charger fans were, so to speak, foaming at the mouth.

Coach Poteete later denied making the comment, though when I asked him about the game and comment during a phone interview he was kind enough to grant, all he would say was, "That was a real good game. Lots of interest. Martin played a real good game."

That's coach-speak that Amos Alonzo Stagg would have been proud of, right there!

Despite the 40-game streak, and despite their record of cardiac comebacks time and again, the media and most fans outside of Martin and Sharon were giving the Chargers very little chance of beating the Rams.

Most outsiders considered that the gig was finally up; the mighty team that had survived on skill and not a little luck was finally meeting an opponent who would get the better of them. Nobody can cheat fate forever. The piper had to be paid, and the bill was due for the Chargers.

Everybody knew that an epic battle was brewing.

I've already set the scene in the book's introduction; in case you have forgotten, maybe you want to glance back there. There were no other local games played that night, as several teams moved their games to Thursday or Saturday so that coaches and players could be in attendance for The Game.

Danny Walker remembers how the hype affected him and his teammates; they'd heard it all week, and were more than ready to get on the field and get things settled. They had arrived at the stadium an hour early to begin warmups. The crowd was filling to capacity, even then, and would soon overflow the stands and see people standing, lined up 6-deep, all the way around the track surrounding the field, to watch.

"I was tired and distracted by the whole thing," Walker said, "and when it was time for us to run a few plays in warmup, I went to my position and put my hands under Johnny Brundige."

Brundige was one of the team's guards, a position that lines up next to the center – in this case, Phil Dane – who is supposed to snap the ball to the quarterback. Walker soon got that bit of confusion straightened out, and the warmups continued.

Jim Graves, the former Martin coach whose 1967 team had started the streak by going 11-0, brought his Union City team to the game that night. When I asked him about it, he said, "Well, I knew we were going to watch two of the best teams in the state that night. I wanted my guys (Union City) to see it."

Then, with just a bit of a gleam in his eye, he said, "Besides – those were my guys (Westview.) I had to be there to pull for them."

Finally, it was time for the kickoff, and for Westview to put the ball in play to Humboldt. If the coach's script played out, the Chargers would get a good, hard defensive stand right off the bat, then the Westview offense would come in for a score and be off to the races.

So much for best laid plans.

Humboldt's Henry Hunt took the kickoff from Johnny Brundige at the 2-yard line and proceeded to motor 98 yards in the other direction for a touchdown. Humboldt missed the point after, and led 6-0. Many of the estimated 10,000 fans were there for Westview, so things got real quiet, real fast.

On the sideline, Danny Walker said that Coach Dunn was reflecting the mood of the crowd, looking at him and mouthing the words, "What are we going to do now?"

Walker assured his coach, "Don't worry; we'll be okay."

And with that, Walker led his team back out and proceeded to score on a 6-yard run himself, knotting the score at 6-6. Charger fans breathed a little easier; maybe it wasn't going to be a blowout, after all.

Humboldt had an All-State running back named Charles Ford, and they threw Ford at the Westview defense with a vengeance. Ford was successful, but Westview soon zoned in on him and began to slow the great back down. The Humboldt drive appeared about to stall at the Westview 37-yard line.

It was then that Humboldt cooked up an end-around play with their lumbering tight end, McCaslin. When the hefty player got up a head of steam, he was hard to stop, and one after one, the Charger players flung themselves at him – to no avail.

Defensive back Don "Duck" Jacobs had one last chance to stop McCaslin, but, as he tells it, "I hit him with everything I had – and then, next thing I knew, I was on my back watching him roll on into the end zone."

Humboldt 14, Westview 6.

42-0

The fury only intensified in the second quarter, as both sides delivered hit after hit. Tim Prince delivered an especially effective thump to a Humboldt running back, and the Chargers seemed to pick up new life. They drove down the field and found themselves at the Humboldt 23-yard line.

What happened next was vintage Danny Walker, according to his teammates – who never quite stood in awe of him, but all of whom agreed with Barry Buckley's assessment: "There was one and only one reason we ever played as well as we did: Danny Walker."

Walker came to the huddle and began to draw a play up on the grass.

(I witnessed him recreate the play while having a conversation over breakfast at the Hearth Restaurant in Martin; he used salt and pepper shakers, along with coffee cups and a syrup bottle to represent his teammates.)

> "Ricky (Wilson) – I want you to go here, and give me a good fake to the outside. Mark (Stafford), I want you to drag back along across the middle and I'm going to hit you with the ball."

The play worked to perfection, and Stafford was in for six points. Walker ran for the conversion, and the score was tied 14-14.

Just before halftime, Ronnie Shanklin took the ball in from 2 yards out, and Westview held the advantage 20-14. During the third quarter, both defenses took center stage, swapping "3 and outs" and fumble recoveries – so that no one scored in that quarter.

As the fourth quarter began, you could feel the swell in the crowd, sensing that an epic finish lay ahead.

Humboldt's offense roused on a 77-yard drive that lasted 9 plays. It was the all-stater, Ford, who took the ball in for the score, knotting the count at 20-20. Barry Buckley delivered a key hit to deny the extra point and preserve the tie with less than 5 minutes left in the game.

What comes next is the stuff that movie endings are made of.

After the Rams held Westview one more time, Rick Wilson uncorked a bomb of a punt – 50 yards to the Humboldt 4-yard line. The Charger defense did its job and held Humboldt, forcing a punt from them. With a great rush that hurried the Humboldt kicker, the ball only traveled to the Ram 35-yard line.

With approximately 2:00 left to go in the game, in came Walker and his troops. There were no overtime rules in high school football in

42-0

those days, so unless the Chargers could score, the game would end in a tie and their "victory" streak would be snapped.

Of course, Humboldt was hoping for a turnover or a quick hold of the Charger offense, desperate to get the ball back and get one more try of their own.

The Charger offense – which had become known for its variations on both power and finesse – went back to piece of sage advice offered by more than one old crusty coach: "You need to dance with the one that brung you."

That meant five straight running plays to Ronnie Shanklin, he of the 2,000 yards and recently-installed gold shoes.

Rick Wilson remembers the calls in the huddle: "Power right, on 2; power left, on 2; power right on 1; power left on 2."

Shanklin went for 9, 6, 15, 5, and – finally – for 2 yards. With :08 seconds left on the clock, Danny Walker called time out, and headed for the sideline.

When asked what his strategy had been on that final drive, Walker responded – "I don't really know; don't fumble the ball, I guess."

After conversing briefly with Coach Dunn, the call went out for the field goal unit.

Johnny Brundige had kicked precisely one field goal all year for the Chargers. Phil Dane, the center and long-snapper on field goal tries, remembers that they had hardly even practiced field goal attempts. It just wasn't part of the normal plan of attack for the Chargers.

> (Johnny told me, "Well, maybe the team never practiced that kick very much – but I did. I had made it a hundred times in my mind. I kicked every single day of the year, even on Christmas.")

Preparing for the field goal attempt, what happened on the Charger sideline can only be described as chaos. Don Jacobs remembers, "We were all running around, and I was trying to find the kicking tee; Johnny was hollering, 'Where's my glasses! Where's my glasses!' There was a lot of shuffling that had to go on, since Johnny was normally a blocker on the line, but of course, he now had to kick the ball."

Jacobs, by the way, was assigned as the holder for the kick; he had to get into the game – hopefully with the tee – and get in position to take the snap from the center.

That center was, as previously mentioned, Phil Dane. Phil remembers, "We didn't know what was going on. Everybody was running around, and I didn't even know we were getting ready for a field goal."

Now, remember, even though Westview had taken a time out, that time out only lasts for so long. After 60 seconds, your team must be properly lined back up on the field, ready to go ahead with the next play. A referee keeps this time on a stopwatch and, for the Chargers, time was running short.

Added to the confusion was the fact that Terry Brockwell – one of Westview's best and fiercest players on defense – was the designated player to enter the game and take Johnny Brundige's place at guard on the line. (Remember, Brundige is lining up to kick the ball.)

The only problem was, Brockwell had broken his leg earlier in the game, and was sitting on the bench (he refused to go into the locker room for treatment.) There was no one to take Johnny Brundige's place, and there was a gaping hole right in front of the Humboldt defender, who was poised to break through and block the kick.

None of the coaches or other players saw what was happening, with the exception of Barry Buckley, who looked out and saw there was nobody in the gap. So, Buckley inserted himself, running onto the field and jumping into Brockwell's spot, yelling at Phil Dane – "what do I do? What do I do?"

With time counting down and the crowd roaring to its feet, Jacobs called for the snap. Phil Dane said, "I was so fired up by this time, that I nearly snapped the ball over Duck's head."

Buckley was still yelling, "What do I do?" when the ball flew back, the defenders rushed in, and the fate of the game hung on Johnny Brundige's big toe.

I remember the moment from my safe perch in the pep band; it seemed as if time slowed down while the ball spun lazily, end over end, toward the goal post. When it "split the upright" – which is football-speak meaning that the kick was good – our band director, Mr. Wilson, immediately hit the cue for the school fight song.

I began blowing my horn as hard and as loud as I could – all my bandmates were doing the same – and then I realized that I couldn't hear a note. Not one sound from the pep band. And, in the next second, I realized that that was because the roar of the crowd was so thunderous that nothing else could be heard.

Westview 23, Humboldt 20 as time expired.

The Streak was now 41-0.

I have never witnessed another game like it in my life.

42-0

Chapter 10: One More – and an Epilogue

The final game of the 1970 season was a renewal of one of the oldest rivalries for both Martin and Sharon; the Yellowjackets of Greenfield.

It's not really fair to say that the game had the feel of an afterthought, or an anti-climax. It was a solid victory for this Charger team of destiny, as they put Greenfield down by a score of 45-14.

This proved to be the final game of the season, as Westview – despite going 10-0 and extending their win streak to 42 games – was not invited into postseason play.

Things were changing on the high school sports scene, and this was the first year of a trial playoff system. Somehow, the Chargers were deemed not to have had enough points to keep playing.

So, that was it.

Ed Chenette, who covered The Streak so faithfully, and from whom we have already heard a number of times, wrote this:

Friday night, another local high school football season came to an end, and to say it was much similar to those of seasons past would be both true and misleading.

It was the same in one all-important respect: for the fourth consecutive year, it was an all-victorious affair, ten games played and ten games won. This is perfection, and better than that no one can get....

Yes, this was a great year, the same as the others in the sense that again the games were played and won; but, also unlike in that the challenges met were even greater, but they were surmounted nevertheless.

A fourth straight all-victorious season? Impossible.

Break the 37-game win streak? Impossible.

Beat Humboldt? Impossible.

But not to the Chargers of Westview.

For, you see, to them, since there is no such word as IMPOSSIBLE, all things are POSSIBLE."

Thanks, Mr. Chenette; I couldn't have said it better myself.

Epilogue

In the first football game of the 1971 season, Union City finally brought the long Martin/Westview winning streak to a close, defeating the Chargers on their own home field. The opposing coach was Jim Graves – who had started the streak five years earlier.

There seems a certain poetic justice in that – perhaps a gift from the football gods.

Coach Graves was not through with Westview; in 1975, after concluding his tenure in Union City, he rejoined the faculty of Westview High School as mathematics teacher and head football coach. It was my distinct honor to be a senior on that team, and to get the opportunity to play for a remarkable man.

Our team was not undefeated that season, but we did win 7 games – the only other winning season in the decade of the 1970's – and second only to that 10-0 team that finished the streak.

The following season, in 1976, Coach Graves led an upstart Charger team to Milan, where the Bulldogs had ascended to the #1 ranking in the state. My brother and his comrades won that game, carrying Coach Graves off the field on their shoulders.

John Fairless

All in all, I'd say it couldn't have happened to a nicer guy.

42-0

A Picture Gallery

Photos are gratefully reprinted here with the permission of the *Weakley County Press*. We regret that original photos from the time are not available, and neither are the negatives. These are taken from press clippings and the morgue file at the paper's Martin, Tennessee office.

Gene Leonard gains some tough yardage; Panthers in the picture are Ricky Chandler, Bobby Morrison, and Johnny Shanklin (Martin v. Lake County, 1968)

Johnny Shanklin for the winning score (Martin v. Trenton, 1968)

Bobby Morrison breaks loose from a defender for 6 points (Martin v. Gleason, 1968)

42-0

Danny Walker scoots around end (Martin v. Greenfield, 1968)

Coach Jimmy Dunn in a familiar pose on the sideline (1969)

Rick Wilson prepares to haul in a Danny Walker pass
(Martin v. Obion Central, 1969)

Team photo of the final Martin Panther football team (1969)
Scrapbook credit: Vicki Redmon

42-0

Panther Cheerleaders were always a plus (l. to r.) Debbie Buchanan, Vickie Redmon, Carol White, Janet Wilkinson, Susan Beeler, Brenda Whitlow, and Donna Williams (Martin v. Trenton, 1969)

UC quarterback John Drerup went for 69 yards and a TD on this play. The slippery white cleats didn't help the Chargers! (Westview v. Union City, 1970)

Terry Brockwell and David Maness make the tackle, with help from Robert Starr, Joel Clements, and Mark Stafford. (Westview vs. Lake County, 1970)

This Duck can fly! Don Jacobs intercepts a pass against the Rebels (Westview v. Henry County, 1970)

42-0

Ronnie Shanklin goes head-to-head with a Milan defender. Do NOT try this at home – or anywhere else, for that matter!
(Westview v. Milan, 1970)

A portion of the record crowd at UTM field – estimated 10,000
(Westview v. Humboldt, 1970)

Both teams were keyed and the action came fast and hot
(Westview v. Humboldt, 1970)

A view of the visitor's sideline and the Ram lineup
(Westview v. Humboldt, 1970)

42-0

Ronnie Shanklin gained tough yardage all night, with the aid of blockers like Mike Nanney (#65)

Everybody waited to see if the kick would be good

(Westview v. Humboldt, 1970)

It Was!

The scoreboard told the final story
(Westview v. Humboldt, 1970)

ABOUT THE AUTHOR

John Fairless grew up in Martin, Tennessee, a graduate of Westview High School and the University of Tennessee at Martin.

www.ingramcontent.com/pod-product-compliance
Lightning Source LLC
Chambersburg PA
CBHW070256100426
42743CB00011B/2249